SING through the DAY

SING

the plough publishing house
Rifton, New York

through the DAY

NINETY SONGS FOR YOUNGER CHILDREN

Compiled and edited by the SOCIETY OF BROTHERS

Music arranged by Marlys Swinger
Illustrated by Jeanie, Joanie and Judy
Music and words hand-lettered by Gillian Barth

First Printing,	1968
Second Printing,	1969
Third Printing,	1971
Fourth Printing,	1976
Fifth Printing,	1986

ISBN 0-87486-107-1
Library of Congress Catalog Card Number 68-9673
Printed by Friesen Printers, Manitoba, Canada

Acknowledgements

The Society of Brothers is grateful for the permission granted in the use of the material which follows. Every effort has been made to locate all sources, and in some cases these could not be found. Any corrections necessary will be made in future editions of this book.

Special thanks are due to the British Broadcasting Corporation, the British Museum, Evans Brothers Limited, Jonathan Cape Limited, the Music Publishers' Association Limited, and the National Christian Education Council for their efforts in helping us locate sources of certain English songs; also to Dr. Percy M. Young for his kind assistance.

"Birthday Presents" from *The Whole World Singing*, compiled by Edith Lovell Thomas; reprinted by permission of the Friendship Press, New York. Copyright 1950.

"Boats Sail on the Rivers" from *Sing-Song* by Christina Rossetti. Reprinted with permission of the Macmillan Company. Copyright 1924 by the Macmillan Company.

"Bumblebees Are Humming," "Dance, Little Maiden," "Dearest Sun" ("Sun Song"), and "Pit, Pat, Pat" ("Home in the Rain"), from *Children's Sing-Song from Sweden* by Alice Tegner, translated into English by Maisie Radford, published by Augener, London. By permission of Galaxy Music Corp., New York, for Galliard, Ltd., London.

"Corn in the Wind" by Rodney Bennett and Joan Bennett from *Child Education*; reprinted by permission of Joan Bennett.

"Daisies" by Frank Dempster Sherman, reprinted and set to music by permission of the Houghton Mifflin Company.

"Easter Greeting" by Laura E. Richards, reprinted by permission of Allenson and Company, London.

"The Fairy Flute" and "Singing Time" by Rose Fyleman, reprinted and set to music by permission of the Society of Authors as literary representative of the Estate of the late Rose Fyleman.

"Firefly" from *Under the Tree* by Elizabeth Madox Roberts. Copyright 1922 by B. W. Huebsch, Inc., 1950 by Ivor S. Roberts. Reprinted by permission of the Viking Press, Inc. The combination of words and music is by Edith Lovell Thomas from *The Whole World Singing*, Friendship Press.

"For the Golden Corn" by E. Gould and E. Smith, and "O Dandelion, Yellow as Gold" by Noreen Bath, from *Child Education*; reprinted by permission of Evans Brothers Limited.

"Go to Bethlehem," "Heaven's Gate Has Opened," and "Up, Little Hans," reprinted by permission of the Cooperative Recreation Service, Inc., Delaware, Ohio.

"Go to Sleep" from *Folk Jingles of American Children* by Dorothy G. M. Howard (Doctoral Dissertation, School of Education, New York University, 1938). Used by permission of Dr. Howard.

"God Made the Shy, the Wild Ones" ("Elizabeth's Carol") by Elizabeth Gould and Hugh S. Roberton, reprinted by permission of J. Curwen and Sons, Ltd., copyright 1951.

"Good Evening, Shining Silver Moon" ("The Moon"), "The Magic Pony," and "The Obedient Kitten" from *A Child's Book of Songs*, copyright 1928; used by permission of the American Book Company.

"The House of the Mouse" from *Another Here and Now Story Book* by Lucy Sprague Mitchell. Copyright 1937 by E.P. Dutton & Co., Inc. Renewal copyright 1965 by Lucy Sprague Mitchell. Reprinted and set to music by permission of the publishers.

"I Am Quite Big" ("Playmates") from *Sixty Songs for Little Children* and "Squirrel Nutkin" from *Second Sixty Songs for Little Children*, reprinted by permission of the Oxford University Press.

"I Held a Lamb" by Kim Worthington, reprinted and set to music by permission of *Child Life*, copyright 1954.

"I'm Little White Clover" ("Song of the White Clover Fairy") from *Flower Fairies of the Summer* by Cicely M. Barker and Olive Linnell. Reprinted by permission of the publisher, Blackie and Son, Ltd.

"Indian Harvest" from *Rhythms and Rimes* of *The World of Music* series. Copyright 1936, 1943, by Ginn and Company. Used with permission.

"Indian Lullaby" by Walter H. Aiken. Reprinted by permission of the Willis Music Company.

"Little Donkey Close Your Eyes" (abridged) from *The Fish with the Deep Sea Smile* by Margaret Wise Brown, published by

Acknowledgements

E.P. Dutton and Co., Inc., copyright 1938 and 1956 by Roberta B. Rauch.

"Little Red Bird" used by permission of Stainer and Bell, London, and the Galaxy Music Corporation.

"Mary's Lullaby" by Ivy O. Eastwick. Reprinted and set to music by special permission of the author and *Jack and Jill* Magazine, copyright 1947, The Curtis Publishing Company.

"Mud" by Polly Chase Boyden from *Child Life* Magazine, copyright 1930, 1958 by Rand McNally & Company. Reprinted and set to music by permission of the publisher and Barbara Boyden Jordan, the author's representative.

"Oro, My Little Boat" from the record *So Early in the Morning* collected by Diane Hamilton, Tradition Record: TLP 1034. By permission of the Everest Record Group, Los Angeles.

"Shepherds Come A-Running" from *A Book of Christmas Carols*, selected and illustrated by Haig & Regina Shekerjian. Arranged for piano by Robert de Cormier. Copyright 1963 by Haig & Regina Shekerjian. Used by permission of Harper & Row, Publishers.

"Song of the Bunnies" from the book *Nibble Nibble* by Margaret Wise Brown, published by Young Scott Books, copyright October 1959; by permission of Jeanne Hale, literary agent for the author.

"The Sun" by John Drinkwater, reprinted and set to music by permission of the Houghton Mifflin Company.

"The Sun Is Rising Out of Bed" ("Morning Song"), words by John Ferguson to an English folk tune, from *Together We Sing*, Follett Publishing Company, copyright 1952. Used with permission.

"This is the Day" used by permission of the composer, T. Janet Surdam. Copyright 1953.

"Three Kings" from *God's Wonderful World* by Agnes Leckie Mason and Phyllis Brown O'Hanian. Copyright 1954 by Agnes Leckie Mason and Phyllis Brown O'Hanian. Reprinted by permission of Random House, Inc.

"To Bethlehem I Would Go" from *Seven Czechoslovak Carols*, published by Schott & Company, Ltd., copyright 1942. Permission granted by Schott & Company, Ltd., and Associated Music Publishers, Inc.

The following songs are published for the first time in English, having been translated from the German by members of the Society of Brothers.

"Dainty Little Butterfly" ("Schmetterling und Blume"), "The Easter Hare" ("Vom Osterhaas"), and "Marie in the Meadow" ("Klein Marie") from *Hundert Kinderlieder* by Edwin Kunz. Reprinted by permission of Orell Füssli Verlag, Zürich.

"The Earth Needs the Raindrops" ("Die Erde braucht Regen") from *Bruder Singer* published by Bärenreiter-Verlag, Kassel and Basel.

"Good Morning, Dear Children" ("Guten Morgen, mein Liebchen") by Walter Rein in *Unser Fröhlicher Gesell*. Reprinted by permission of Möseler Verlag, Wolfenbüttel, who hold all rights. Copyright 1956.

"Sunshine and Rain" ("Sonne und Regen müssen ja sein") by Margarete Derlien. Reprinted by permission of Bärenreiter-Verlag, Kassel and Basel, who hold all rights.

For everyone who has a childlike heart

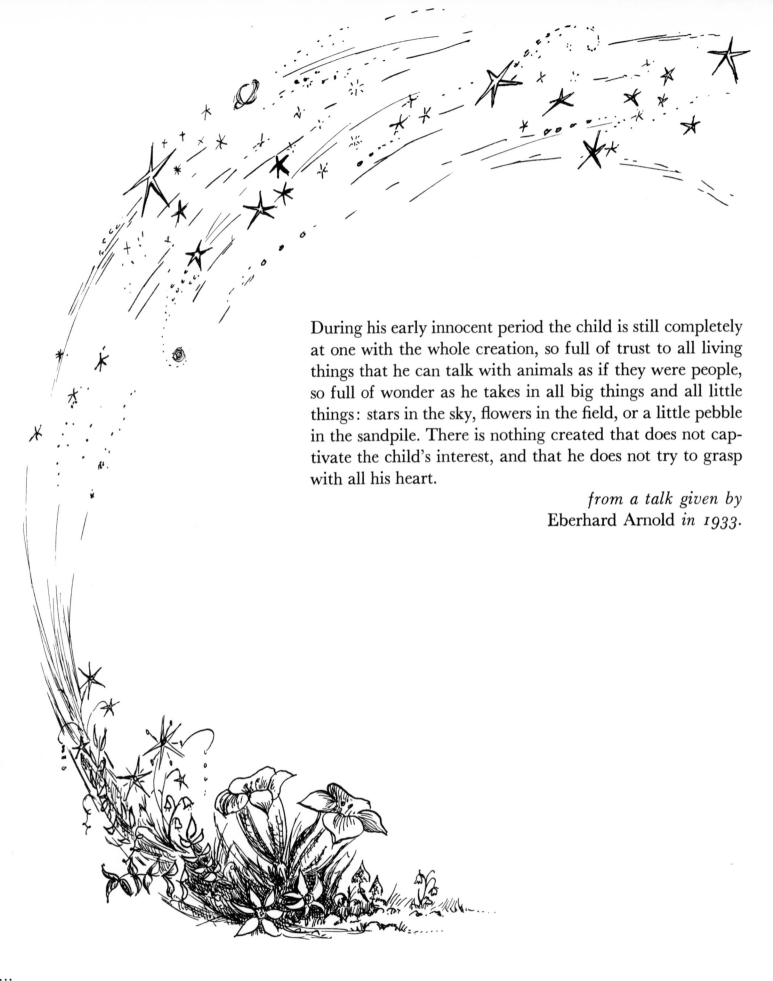

During his early innocent period the child is still completely at one with the whole creation, so full of trust to all living things that he can talk with animals as if they were people, so full of wonder as he takes in all big things and all little things: stars in the sky, flowers in the field, or a little pebble in the sandpile. There is nothing created that does not captivate the child's interest, and that he does not try to grasp with all his heart.

from a talk given by
Eberhard Arnold *in 1933.*

Introduction

Do you like to sing with children? We do! And because we would like to share the songs we have been singing with our children through the years, we've made a book, including many of our favorites.

This collection of songs comes out of the community life of a group known as the Society of Brothers. In these communities, families and single people live together in a life of full sharing, based on the example of the early Christians. The Society makes its home in three places in the United States: Rifton, New York; Farmington, Pennsylvania; and Norfolk, Connecticut,[1] and in one place in England: Darvell, Robertsbridge, Sussex.

In these four[2] communities, the children spend a part of each day with other children of their age group and share many experiences together. These groups range from younger children through the eighth grade. It is natural for our children to sing together (one of the favorites of the youngest is "Hallelujah" on page 117), and all the everyday times—morning, play-time, mealtimes, going-to-bed—bring tunes and words to their lips.

Parents share closely with their children and the teachers in all that they experience through the daily life in the community. (A fuller picture of the life of our children is given in the book *Children in Community*.)

Some of the songs in this book (for example, "Dwarf Song" and "The Princess Was a Lovely Child") have been sung since the beginning years of our life together, dating back to the early 1920's in Germany. At this time a small number of people, under the guidance of Eberhard Arnold, chose to live together in a life of love and service as a witness to brotherhood. Other individuals and families came to join with the

---

[1]Also in Ulster Park, New York
[2]Now five.

first few in this life of searching together. In time, after much hardship and struggle, a farm was purchased. This community was forced to leave Germany in the late 1930's because of the persecution from the Nazis and for a time made its home in England. From there, another forced exodus was made to Paraguay, the only country which would immediately accept immigrants during war time. (The story of the beginning years of the community is told in the book, *Torches Together,* by Emmy Arnold.)

Throughout all the years of moving about and of living and discovering together, our lives have been enriched by song. As people of various nationalities and from all walks of life have joined us, the songs have become increasingly varied. Also new songs have been written through special occasions or experiences—a song for a new baby, a new birthday song, or one for a festive occasion. The songs in this book are both old and new, but all belong to the experience of the childlike heart. Because we feel celebrations and festivals are so very special, we wanted to share with you some favorite songs from these occasions. They are grouped together in the back of the book under the title song, "This Is the Day," which in itself is a song for a special day.

Three of our college-age girls have done the illustrations, thinking especially of what children would like (notice the shepherds and wise men portrayed as children in the Christmas section). It is our hope that the pictures and songs will make a book that will be most useful and most enjoyable, and that whoever you are—parent, teacher, grandparent, or lover-of-children—you will join voices with the children and "Sing Through the Day."

Marlys Swinger

Contents

THE SUN IS RISING OUT OF BED

COME OUT AND PLAY

Songs appearing in print for the first time are designated "*Original*."

GOD MADE THE SHY, THE WILD ONES

DANCE TO THE MERRY PIPER'S SOUND

PIT, PAT, PAT

GOOD EVENING

THIS IS THE DAY!

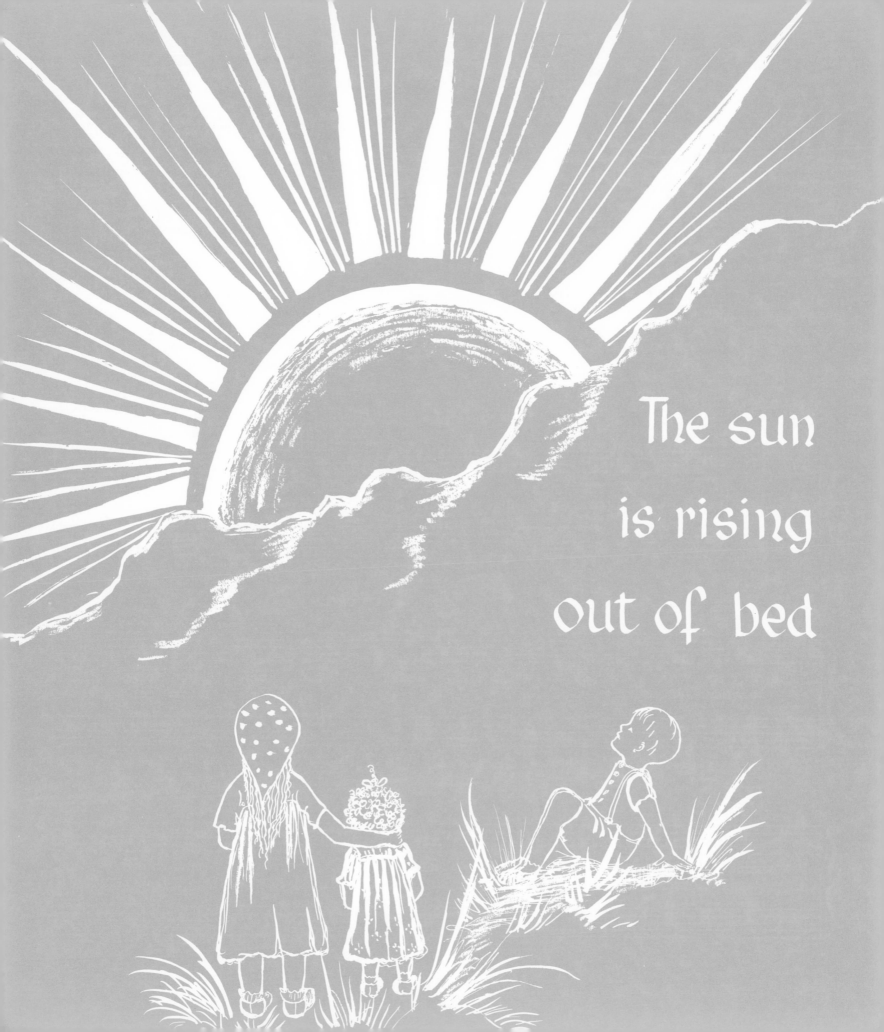

The sun
is rising
out of bed

The Sun Is Rising Out of Bed

John Ferguson

English Folk Tune

Fast and lively

1. The sun is ris-ing out of bed, And in the East the sky is red; Then up and wake each sleep-y-head, So ear-ly in the morn-ing. 'Tis shame to dream the hours a-way, When all the world is bright with day, And

2. The light is clear on hill and lea, The birds are loud in ev-'ry tree; Then haste and rise and come with me, So ear-ly in the morn-ing. With pleas-ant sights and sounds to spare, With hearts a-lert and free from care, We'll

Na-ture calls to work or play, So ear-ly in the morn-ing.
out and drink the whole-some air, So ear-ly in the morn-ing.

3. Where 'neath the share the furrows gleam,
We'll see the ploughman drive his team,
Or wander down beside the stream,
So early in the morning.
And where the water's fresh and cool,
We'll watch the trout within the pool;
There's time before we go to school,
So early in the morning.

3

Dearest Sun

Maisie Radford (English translation from Swedish)   Alice Tegner

Cheerfully

Dear-est sun, if you warm us Nei-ther cold nor frost can harm us. Shine on
Dear-est sun, come and cheer us And the grass and bush-es near us. Let us

fa-ther and mo-ther and my great big bro-ther And my sis-ter tall,___ Shine
see you shine o-ver sheep and kine, O-ver horse and mill, O-ver

on us all. Shine the whole day-time through And please come back to-mor-row too!
vale and hill, O-ver land, o-ver sea And where-so-ev-er we may be!

Good Morning, Dear Children

Walter Rein

3 Part Round

Good morn-ing! Good morn-ing! Good morn-ing, dear chil-dren. Come out-side now, it is

time now, Come out-side now, leave your hous-es, For the sun, for the sun, for the sun's in the sky.

The Rooster's
Our Watchman

Thuringian Folk Song

Merrily

1. The roos-ter's our watch-man, The lord of the farm is he, The lord of the
2. His crest is so hand-some, He looks like a king so grand, He looks like a

farm. / king. He wakes us both sum-mer and win-ter so ear-ly With crow-ing so lus-ty, with

*ki - ke - ri - ki - ki! Sing-ing tral-le-ra, **vi-de-ral-le-ra, Sing-ing tral-le-ra, vi-de-

ral-le-ra, With a ***ruk - ke - tuk - ke and a ruk - ke - tuk - ke, Sing-ing ki - ke-ri- ki - ki!

3. With spurs on his two heels
   He's proud as a knight who rides,
   He's proud as a knight . . .

*   pronounced: kee - kuh - ree - kee - kee
**   vee - duh - ral - le - ra
***   rook - uh - took - uh

Come Arise!

2 Part Round

Johann Jacob Wachsmann

1. Come a - rise, come a - rise! The cock doth crow;

2. The sun on his gold - en path doth go.

Alpine Song

Swiss Folk Song

Very gay

1. Long be-fore the ris-ing sun Has his mer-ry work be-gun, Swift I climb the up-land mead-ow, Heed not frost nor moun-tain shad-ow With my cows on moun-tain height There is my de-light.___ Ho-a, ho-a, *ho di-di, Ho di-ri di,

2. Come my cows, come Spiess and Star, Young ones, old ones, near and far; Look, I have no stick to beat you; I have on-ly salt to treat you, Come now quick-ly when I call, I have hay for all.___

*ho-dee-dee, Ho-dee-ree-dee

8

Ho di-ri di, Ho-a, ho-a, ho di-di, Ho di-ri di, di-ri di.

3 Hear the milkmaids one and all
Singing as the echoes call.
They can milk and they can churn;
They can make the butter turn;
All their work is their delight
On the mountain height.

The Merry Little Robin

Nursery Song

Gently

D   G   D   A⁷   D

There came to my win-dow one morn-ing in spring A sweet lit-tle rob-in, she came there to sing; The
Her wings she was spread-ing to soar far a-way, Then rest-ing a mom-ent seemed sweet-ly to say : "Oh

G   D   A⁷   D

tune that she sang, it was pret-ti-er far Than an-y I heard on a flute or gui-tar. ___
hap-py, how hap-py the world seems to be, A-wake lit-tle girl, and be hap-py with me!" ___

The Sweet Rosy Morn

Richard Leveridge

Brisk and lively

The sweet ro-sy morn-ing peeps o - ver the hills, With blush-es a-dorn-ing the

mead - ows and fields; ___ The mer-ry, mer-ry, mer-ry horn calls, Come, come, come, a-

way! A - wake from your slum - ber, and hail the new day. ___ The day. ___

Come, Little Sennerin

Swedish Folk Song

Come, lit-tle Sen-ne-rin, Call all the cows in, Put on your shoes, For it's
Hark, can you hear all the cow-bells a-ring-ing? Pull at the rope, Let the

time to go milk-ing; First, milk Dam-e-lin, Ro-sa, Fag-e-lin.
goats all go spring-ing; First, milk Dam-e-lin, Ro-sa, Fag-e-lin.

Tu-tu-tu, the horn calls. Drive them home safe-ly when night falls.

Up, Little Hans!

Danish

Lively

1. "Up, lit-tle Hans! Up, lit-tle Hans! Hear the bird-ies sing-ing!"
2. "Up, lit-tle Hans! Up, lit-tle Hans! Soon will ring the school bell!"

"No, Mom-my, No! No, Mom-my, No! Just the barn door swing-ing!"
"No, Mom-my, No! No, Mom-my, No! I don't feel at all well!"

3. "Up, little Hans!
Up, little Hans!
You may play your drum now!"
"Yes, Mommy, Yes!
Yes, Mommy, Yes!
Yes, I think I'll come now!"

The Sun

John Drinkwater

Marlys Swinger

Cheerily

I told the Sun that I was glad, I'm sure I don't know why; Some-how the pleas-ant

way he had Of shin-ing in the sky,___ Just put a no-tion in my head That

wouldn't it be fun___ If, walk-ing on the

hill, I said "I'm hap-py" to the Sun.

*Instead of "I'm happy," children
may wish to sing "Good morning."

14

Singing Time

Rose Fyleman

Anonymous

I wake in the morn-ing ear - ly___ and al - ways, the ver-y first thing, I

poke out my head and I sit up in bed and I sing and I sing and I sing and I sing and I

sing and I sing,_____ when I

wake in the morn - ing ear - ly.___

There's a Sun for the Morning

Charles Ellerton

Thoughtfully

1. There's a sun for the morn-ing, And a moon for the night; When the
2. Light and warmth, joy and beau-ty Come from God high a-bove, And He

moon hides her face, Still the stars twin-kle bright. When the bright.
gives these good gifts From a heart full of love. And He love.

Attributed to W.A. Mozart

16

Come out

and play

Come Out and Play

The Swing

Robert Louis Stevenson

Unknown

1. How do you like to go up in a swing,— Up in the air so blue?—
2. Up in the air and o - ver the wall,— Till I can see so wide,—

Oh, I do think it the pleas - ant - est thing—
Ri - vers and trees and cat - tle and all—

Ev - er a child can do!———
O - ver the coun - try - side ———

3. Till I look down on the garden green,
Down on the roof so brown—
Up in the air I go flying again,
Up in the air and down!

20

I Am Quite Big, But My Lisbeth Is Wee

Frances B. Wood

German Folk Tune

I am quite big but my Lis - beth is wee,___ Lis - beth is
Dai - sies and but - ter - cups grow in the green,___ grow in the

wee,___ For I am past five and my
green,___ With a gold and white crown I will

Lisbeth's just three.___
make Lis - beth queen.___

Let's Hike to the Woodlands Today

Thuringian Folk Song

Very jolly

1. Let's hike to the woodlands to-day, Hal-lo, hal-li, hal-lo.___ The
2. We'll hunt where the mush-rooms all grow, Hal-lo, hal-li, hal-lo.___ And

ber - ries hang ripe on our way,___ Hal-lo, hal-li, hal-lo.___ Tra-la-la-la-
when we have picked them we'll go,___ Hal-lo, hal-li, hal-lo.___ Tra-la-la-la-

la, tra-la-la-la-la, Tra-la-la-la-la-la-la, tra-la-la-la.

3. We're jolly as elves in the wood,
   Hal-lo, hal-li, hal-lo.
   So merry our feast and so good!
   Hal-lo, hal-li, hal-lo.

23

O Dandelion, Yellow as Gold

Noreen Bath

"O Dan-de-li-on, yel-low as gold, What do you do all day?"___ "I

just wait here in the tall, green grass Till the chil-dren come to play." "O Dan-de-li-on,

yel-low as gold, What do you do all night?"___ "I wait and wait till the cool dew falls And my

hair grows long and white." "And what do you do when your hair is white and the chil-dren come to play?" "They take me up in their dim-pled hands, And blow my hair a-way."

Marie in the Meadow

Johann Trojan

Edwin Kunz

1. Ma - rie in the mead-ow, In the mead-ow Ma - rie, All the flow-ers and
2. Oh, I am so wor - ried, I've lost my Ma - rie; She's lost in the

grass-es are tall - er than she.
clo - ver, Oh, where can she be?

3. But who is it sitting 'mid the flowers so bright,
The harebells, the buttercups, the star daisies white?

4. This can't be a flower, a little head I see, —
I've found her, I've found her, I've found my Marie!

25

The Bicycle

Jane Tyson Clement

Marlys Swinger

Off to an uneven start

It wob-bles and tips, I spill in a pud-dle. It flops on its side, Till I'm

all in a mud-dle. It just won't go straight, the ped-als aren't there where I

want them to be, But most an-y-where.

very smoothly

Then all of a sud-den with-out an-y warn-ing, I

cresc.

know how to ride,___ I know how to ride!___What a glo-ri-ous, glo-ri-ous morn-ing!___

27

The Magic Pony

Robert A. Coan

G. Meyerbeer

Quickly

Come and take a ride with me up-on my mag-ic po-ny!
Up and down the world we'll go with not a thought of dan-ger,

Fast and far we'll trav-el, all the live-long day; He can car-ry
Swift-er than the breez-es blow-ing wild and free; We will see the

two of us, for he is ve - ry strong, So you may come a - long, when I
strang - est sights in Eng - land, France and Spain, And then come home a - gain, when it's

ride a - way! So you may come a - long, when I ride a - way!___
time for tea! And then come home a - gain, when it's time for tea!___

The Fairy Flute

Rose Fyleman

Wolfgang Löwenthal

Smoothly

1. My bro-ther has a lit-tle flute Of gold and i-vo-ry,___ He
2. He plays it ev-'ry morn-ing And ev-'ry af-ter-noon,___ And

found it on a sum-mer night With-in a hol-low tree.___
all the lit-tle sing-ing-birds Lis-ten to the tune.___

3. He plays it in the meadows,
And everywhere he walks
The flowers start a-nodding
And dancing on their stalks.

4. He plays it in the village
And all along the street
The people stop to listen,
The music is so sweet.

5. And none but he can play it
And none can understand,
Because it is a fairy flute
And comes from Fairyland.

30

Dance, Little Maiden

(Translated from Swedish by)
Maisie Radford

Alice Tegner

Lightly

Dance, lit-tle maid-en, Dance up-on the hill-tops, So do the fair-ies dance round the dew-drops!

Let all your steps be ve-ry, ve-ry light, For fair-ies would laugh at a hea-vy sprite!

God made the shy,

the wild ones

God Made the Shy, the Wild Ones

(Elizabeth's Carol)

Elizabeth Gould

Quietly, smoothly

H.S. Roberton

1. God made the shy,— the wild ones Who live in field and wood;—
2. He taught them all— the wis - dom And won - der of— their ways.—

He taught them how— to make their homes, And how to find their food.—
We love to learn a - bout— them, And sing God's love and praise.—

Daintily

Mole and vole and ti-ny mouse, The squirr'l in the tree,___

mp - first time
pp - second time

Rab-bit, hare and hedge-hog, And the birds all fly-ing free.___ free.___

I'm Little White Clover

Cicely Mary Barker

Olive Linnell

I'm lit-tle White Clo-ver, kind and clean, Look at my three-fold leaves of green;

Hark to the buz-zing of hun-gry bees, "Give us your hon-ey, Clo-ver, please!"

Yes, lit-tle bees, and wel-come too! My hon-ey is good and meant for you!

Bumblebees Are Humming

(Translated from Swedish by)
Maisie Radford

Alice Tegner

Bum-ble-bees are hum-ming: hum, hum. Pus-sies beat up-on the drum, drum.

Mice are danc-ing round the room, room. All the world is boom-ing: boom, boom!

The House of the Mouse

Lucy Sprague Mitchell

Marlys Swinger

The house of the mouse is a wee lit-tle house, a green lit-tle house in the grass, which

big clum-sy folk may hunt and may poke and still nev-er see as they pass___ this

sweet lit-tle, neat lit-tle, wee lit-tle, green lit-tle, cud-dle-down hide-a-way house in the grass.___

My New Pet Mouse

Jane Tyson Clement

Marlys Swinger

He wig-gled his whis-kers and looked up at me. Did he won-der if I was a queer kind of tree? He sniffed at my fin-gers and nib-bled my bread, Did he think that he was a - nib-bl - ing me, nib-bl - ing me in-stead? If I stay ve-ry qui-et and speak ve-ry low, Then may-be some morn-ing my mous-ie will know That I'm not good to eat, And I'm not a queer tree,— I'm me!

I Held a Lamb

Kim Worthington

Marlys Swinger

One day when I went vis-it-ing, A lit-tle lamb was there,__ I picked it up and

held it tight, It did-n't seem to care.__ Its wool was soft and felt so warm—like

sun-light on the sand,__ And when I gen-tly put it down It licked me on the hand.__

Dainty Little Butterfly

Wolrad Eigenbrodt

Edwin Kunz

Dain-ty lit-tle but-ter-fly, but-ter-fly, On the pur-ple heath-er;
Dain-ty lit-tle flow-er blue, flow-er blue, Ring your bells so light-ly,

Spread your lit-tle wings and fly in the sky, Wings as blue as heav-en.
That your but-ter-fly will hear and come near, Dain-ty lit-tle flow-er.

Worms

(for Jonny)

Gillian Barth

Marlys Swinger

Why does-n't Mom-my like worms in my pock-et? Not hair-y or scar-y, but squig-gly and
Mom-my says worms like a home in our gar-den—A-lone and un-known in a home 'neath a

wig-gly; I wish I could keep all my worms in my pock-et. But my

stone, so I think I'll put all of my worms in our gar-den.

Squirrel Nutkin

Frances B. Wood

Spanish Folk Tune

Lightly

1. Squir-rel Nut-kin has a coat of brown Quite the love-li-est in Wood-land Town.
2. Squir-rel Nut-kin in his coat of brown Scam-pers up the trees and down,
3. All the live - long__ day he plays In the leaf - y__ wood-land ways;

repeat for v.3 only

1. Two bright eyes look round to__ see__ Where the sweet - est__ nuts may be.__
2. Dash-ing here and swing - ing there, Leap - ing light - ly__ through the air.__
3. { But at night when squir - rels rest__ In a co - sy__ tree - top nest, }
{ Bush-y tail curled round his head, Mis - ter Squirrel goes off to bed. }

Song of the Bunnies

Margaret Wise Brown   Marlys Swinger

Bun-nies zip and bun-nies zoom __
Bun-nies jump and bun-nies run __

Bun-nies some-times sleep till noon __ Zoom Zoom Zoom Zoom __ All through the
Bun-nies al-so sit in the sun __ Run Run Run Run __ Run bun-nies

af-ter-noon __ Zoom Zoom Zoom Zoom __ This is the song of the bun-nies.
jump and run __ Run Run Run Run __ This is the song of the bun-nies.

The Obedient Kitten

French Folk Song

Lively

1. Oh, once there was a maid - en, Sing hey, hey, hey, and a roun-de-lay, Oh, once there was a
2. She made a cheese so tast - y, Sing hey, hey, hey, and a roun-de-lay, She made a cheese so

maid - en, Who watched her sheep all day, they say, Who watched her sheep all day.
tast - y, One sun - ny sum-mer day, they say, One sun - ny sum-mer day.

3. Her kitten sat and watched her,
   Sing hey, hey, hey, and a roundelay,
   Her kitten sat and watched her,
   As any kitten may, they say,
   As any kitten may.

4. "Now, kitty, keep your paws off!"
   Sing hey, hey, hey, and a roundelay,
   "Now, kitty, keep your paws off!
   And see that you obey, I say!
   And see that you obey!"

5. Oh, kitty kept her paws off,
   Sing hey, hey, hey, and a roundelay,
   Oh, kitty kept her paws off,
   She found a better way, they say,
   She found a better way!

Firefly

Elizabeth Madox Roberts

Croatian Air

Whimsically

A lit-tle light is go-ing by, A lit-tle light is go-ing by, Is go-ing up to
I nev-er could have thought of it, I nev-er could have thought of it, To have a lit-tle

see the sky, A lit-tle light with wings.
bug all lit,   And made to go on wings, on wings.

Dance

to the

merry piper's

sound

Dance to the Merry Piper's Sound

Very Gay

Swedish Dance Song

Dance to the mer-ry pip-er's sound, Mu-sic is ver-y gay all a-round,
Sing ev-'ry-one on this mer-ry day, Birds join our hap-py roun-de-lay,

Glad boys and girls are here to be found, While nim-ble feet are danc-ing.___
Fill-ing the air with mus-ic so gay, While nim-ble feet are danc-ing.___

One, two, three, One, two, three, Hap-py are we, Hearts full of glee,

One, two, three, One, two, three, While nim-ble feet are danc-ing.

Oh, We Are Two Musicians

German

The Princess Was a Lovely Child

Old European Singing Game

1. The prin-cess was a love-ly child, love-ly child, love-ly child. The

The princess stands alone in center of circle of children.

prin-cess was a love-ly child, love-ly child.

2. She lived high in a castle tall,
   castle tall, . . .

   Children in the circle unclasp hands and raise them high over their heads.

3. There came a wicked fairy by,
   fairy by, . . .

   Children join hands. Child selected to be the wicked fairy goes around the outside of circle, then enters.

4. "Oh, princess, sleep one hundred years,
   hundred years, . . ."

   Wicked fairy sings and casts spell over the princess who falls asleep. Wicked fairy leaves.

5. A big, high hedge grew all around,
   all around, . . .

   Children in circle, keeping hands joined, raise arms high.

6. A gallant prince came riding by,
   riding by, . . .

   Child selected to be the prince rides around the outside of circle.

7. He chopped the trees down one by one,
   one by one, . . .

   Prince "chops down hedge" by breaking open the joined hands of the children.

8. "Oh, princess, wake and be my bride,
   be my bride, . . .

   Prince enters circle and sings to the princess.

9. So everybody's happy now,
   happy now, . . .

   Prince and Princess dance together, and all the children skip in a circle clapping hands.

53

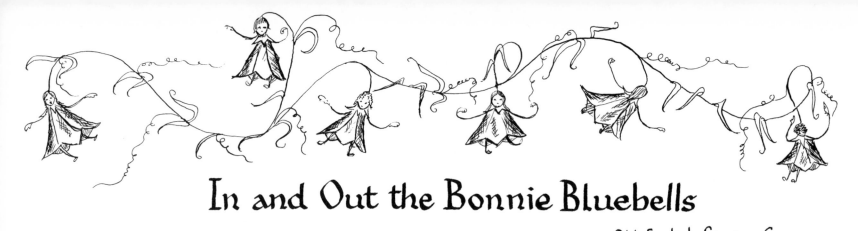

In and Out the Bonnie Bluebells

Old English Singing Game

In and out the bon-nie blue-bells, In and out the bon-nie blue-bells,

Children are in circle, holding joined hands high.
One child who is "It" weaves in and out of circle.

In and out the bon-nie blue-bells, For you are my part-ner.

"It" stops behind another child.

Pit-ta, pat-ta, pit-ta, pat-ta, On your shoul-der, Pit-ta, pat-ta, pit-ta, pat-ta, On your shoul-der,

With both hands "It" taps alternately
on the shoulders of child.

Pit-ta, pat-ta, pit-ta, pat-ta, On your shoul-der, For you are my part-ner.

On the repeat of the dance, the two children ("It" and partner with hands joined) weave in
and out of circle and stop behind two consecutive children. On the next repeat the four
54 *children weave in and out. The dance continues till all children are following "It".*

The Shepherd Maiden

French

I.   D   G   D⁷   G   D   G   D   G

See a *Shep-herd Maid-er here Stand-ing with her sheep so near;___
With a part-ner she will make For the sheep a lit-tle gate.___

*or, "Shepherd Boy is here.."/

II.   D

Run-ning quick-ly they will pass To the up-land mead-ow grass,___
*Shep-herd Maid-en, call them home; Day is done, no more they'll roam;___

*or, "Shepherd Boy now call them,.."

G   D   G   D⁷   G   D⁷   G

Where the past-ure is the best, Till the sun sets in the west.___
Safe with-in the guard-ed fold, Shelt-er them from harm and cold.___

(I)   Shepherd Maiden (or Boy) stands alone in center of a circle of children. Repeat of (I): Shepherdess (or Shepherd) walks to one child at side of circle. Together they make a "gate" by clasping hands and raising them high.

(II): All the sheep go through their gate and "out to pasture." Repeat of (II): All the sheep go back through the gate and "home."

55

The Elfin Cap

German

Very jolly

A-round, a-round our cir-cle runs a point-ed Elf-in Cap, did-dle dum, A-round, a-round our

One child (the Elfin Cap) runs around inside of circle of children.
He puts his palms together over his head to make the "Elfin Cap."

56

cir-cle runs a point-ed Elf-in Cap. Three times three is nine you know,

See the Cap nod to and fro; Add some more then if you will, Elf-in Cap stands still, stands

Elfin Cap nods his head as he runs.

Elfin Cap stops in front of one child.

still, stands still. He jumps to left, he jumps to right, Kicks his heels, it's

Elfin Cap jumps left then right.

He kicks heels behind himself, standing in place.

quite a sight, Then greets the new Elf Cap, Then greets the new Elf Cap.

Elfin Cap greets the new Elf Cap as teacher suggests (hand-shake, bow or curtsey).

57

Cobblers' Dance

Danish

Merrily

Wind, wind, wind the bob-bin, Wind, wind, wind the bob-bin, Pull and pull and tap, tap, tap.

Children are in a circle facing center; they make winding motion with hands for one measure, reversing direction of the winding on the second measure.

Each child pulls elbows back two times.

Tap one fist on other fist three times

Skip-ping round and round we go, Light-ly, light-ly in a row.

Children skip around in a circle.

The Carpenters

South American

With vigor

1. The car-pen-ters are work-ing, Saw-ing the lum-ber. We love to watch them
2. The car-pen-ters are work-ing, Pound-ing the nails in. We love to watch them

Several "carpenters" are in center of circle. They make motions and all the children imitate them.

work-ing, Saw-ing the lum-ber. They go *see*, we go *saw*, They go *see*,
work-ing, Pound-ing the nails in. They go *bang*, we go *clang*, They go *bang*,

we go *saw*, Un-til we've sawed the lum-ber. Fin-ished at last!____
we go *clang*, Un-til we've pound-ed the nails in. Fin-ished at last!____

3. Oh, see the masons working,
    mixing the mortar;
   We love to watch them working,
    mixing the mortar.
   They go *swish*, we go *swoosh*,
   They go *swish*, we go *swoosh*,
   Until we've mixed the mortar.
    Finished at last!

4. Oh, see the masons working,
    putting the bricks in;
   We love to watch them working,
    putting the bricks in;
   They go *clink*, we go *clank*,
   They go *clink*, we go *clank*,
   Until we've put the bricks in.
    Finished at last!

The Little Red Hen

Marlys Swinger

Lively

1. The Lit-tle Red Hen asked the La-zy Three, The Pig and the Dog and the Cat, "Who'll
2. The Lit-tle Red Hen asked the La-zy Three, The Pig and the Dog and the Cat, "Who'll

plant these grains of wheat for me?" "Not I," said each of the La-zy Three, The
cut this love-ly wheat for me?" "Not I," said each of the La-zy Three, The

60

Pig and the Dog and Cat._____ So the Lit-tle Red Hen with a chuck-le of glee plant-ed
Pig and the Dog and Cat._____ So the Lit-tle Red Hen with a chuck-le of glee cut

all the wheat with a fa - la - lee, Now what do you think of that?_____
all the wheat with a fa - la - lee, Now what do you think of that?_____

3...."Who'll take this wheat to the mill for me?"
....took the wheat to the mill with a fa-la-lee...

4...."Who'll make this flour into bread for me?"
....made the flour into bread with a fa-la-lee...

5. The Little Red Hen asked the Lazy Three,
The Pig and the Dog and the Cat,
"Who'll eat those loaves of bread with me?"
"I WILL," said each of the Lazy Three,
The Pig and the Dog and Cat.
But the Little Red Hen with a chuckle of glee
Ate all the bread with a fa-la-lee,
Now what do you think of that?

Dwarf Song

Secretly   German

Deep in the cav-erns of our moun-tain, Rum-pe-di, Pum-pe-di, Rum-pe-di, Pum-pe-di,

Children walk around in a circle, bent over like dwarfs carrying a bag over-shoulder.

Dwell the dwarfs, those bu-sy lit-tle peo-ple, Who do the work for kind-heart-ed folk.

1. Of-ten they sweep with a ti-ny broom,
2. And when the cows in the sta-ble stand,
3. And in the night when the ba-by cries,

Nix, Nax, Nix, Nax, Nox,

Clean-ing the kitch-en and
They'll do the milk-ing with
Gent-ly they'll rock till a-

Children imitate dwarfs in acting each verse.

ev-'ry room,
nim-ble hand,
sleep it lies,

Nix, nax, Nix, nax, nox, Nick, nack, nox, Nick, nack, nox, Nick, nack, nick, nack, Nick, nack, nox.

Corn in the Wind

Rodney Bennett

Joan Bennett

Swayingly

Our hands are ears of corn,_____ Gold-en wav-ing corn,_____ And when winds

blow,_____ The oth-er way they go._____ *Wind speaks loudly:*

"I am the West Wind." The west winds blow!
"I am the East Wind." The east winds blow!

Whoo! Whoo! Whoo! Whoo!

O-ver to east we go._____
O-ver to west we go._____
That is the way the corn ears go When the Four Winds blow._____

One child takes the part of the wind. The others face north, raise hands above heads, constantly flutter their fingers and sing the first eight measures.(They are not sung again.) Children drop hands while Wind runs up on the west side and speaks, "I am the West Wind."

Children sing the rest of the song, bending over to the east on the first count of each measure as the Wind says, "Whoo!"
Repeat, with Wind running around to the other side and becoming the East Wind, then the South, then the North Wind. (Or a different child could be each different Wind.)

64

Pit, pat, pat,

go the Little

wet

feet

Pit, Pat, Pat

Translated from Swedish by
Maisie Radford

Alice Tegner

Pit, pat, pat, go the lit-tle wet feet, Pit, pat, pat, pit, pat, pat. To be
boots soon dry when the sun comes out, Sun comes out, sun comes out;

out in the rain, what a treat, treat, treat. Pit, pat, pat. For the
Mo-ther is wait-ing and hears us shout, Hears us shout. When we

wet, for the wet does the chil-dren good, Chil-dren good, chil-dren good, When they
come in at last from our long, long day, long, long day, long, long day, We get

sing as they walk as all chil-dren should, Chil-dren should. Our
brown bread and but-ter and curds and whey, Curds and whey.

Who Loves the Wind on a Stormy Night

Anonymous

Mysteriously

1. Who loves the wind on a storm-y night, When cur-tains are drawn and

fires are bright? He roars down the chim-ney, the win-dows he shakes, And all round the house such an up-roar he makes,___ Ooh___

dim.   *mp*

Ooh___   Ooh___   says the wind.

2. He rocks the nests in the tree-tops high
And blows the kites right up in the sky;
He fills the sails of the ships so fine
And dries the washing hung out on the line.
Ooh__, Ooh__, Ooh__, says the wind.

3. When snowdrops make their bravest show
And cold March winds begin to blow,
We know that in spite of the wind and the rain
That summer will soon be here again.
Ooh__, Ooh__, Ooh__, says the wind.

69

Rain in the Night

Amelia Josephine Burr

Marlys Swinger

Lightly

Hear it rain-ing, rain-ing, rain-ing, Hear it rain-ing all night long; It is
There'll be ri-vers in the gut-ters And lakes a-long the street. It will

First time - Staccato;
Second time - Legato

some-times loud and some-times soft, And some-times like a song.____
make our la-zy kit-ty Wash his lit-tle dir-ty feet.____

The ro-ses will wear dia-monds Like kings and queens at court;____ But the

pan-sies all get mud-dy Be-cause they are so short. I will sail my boat to-mor-row__ In won-der-ful new plac - es, But first I'll take my wat-'ring pot And

wash the pan-sies' fa - ces,__ And wash the pan-sies' fa - ces.

Hi, Thunder!

Vigorously

Hi, Thun-der! 'Lo, Thun-der! Thun-der on the moun-tain, Thun-der in the val-ley, Thun-der in my
Hi, Sun! 'Lo, Sun! Sun-shine on the moun-tain, Sun-shine in the val-ley, Sun-shine in my

room, Oh, come and play with us. *(spoken)* Well! The thun-der went a-way And the
room, Oh, come and play with us. Well! The sun-shine's not a-round And I

sun came out to play. *(1.)* *(2.)* hear the Thun-der sound! Hi, Thun-der! 'Lo, Thun-der! Thun-der on the moun-tain,

Thun-der in the val-ley, Thun-der in my room, Oh, come and play with us.

Words and music by
the children of the
Macedonia Community

72

Mud!

Polly Chase Boyden

Marlys Swinger

Mud is ve-ry nice to feel All squish-y-squash be-tween the toes! I'd

rath-er wade in wig-gly mud Than smell a yel-low rose.____ No-

bod-y else but the rose-bush knows How nice mud feels be-tween the toes.

Boats Sail on the Rivers

Christina Rossetti

Marlys Swinger

Smoothly

Boats sail on the ri - vers, And ships sail on the seas;___ But clouds that sail a-

cross the sky Are pret-ti-er far than these.___ There are brid-ges on the ri - vers, As

pret-ty as you please; But the bow that brid - ges heav - en, And o - ver-tops the

trees, And builds a road from earth to sky, Is pret-ti-er far than these.___

Oro, My Little Boat

Irish Folk Song

Flowing

1. O - ro, my lit - tle boat that rests in the bay, O - ro ma var - din,
2. Sail - ing the waves o - ver foam-white crests, O - ro ma var - din,
3. Rid - ing the waves on the o - cean's rim, O - ro ma var - din,

Take up the oars and let us a - way, O - ro ma var - din.
Hap - py and free a - way to the west, O - ro ma var - din.
Sail - ing home as the light grows dim, O - ro ma var - din.

O - ro ma *cur-ra-agh O, O - ro ma var - din,

O - ro ma cur-ra-agh O, O - ro ma var - din.

*pronounced: Koor-ra-kee no

76

Sunshine and Rain

Words from
Lithuanian Folk Song

Margarete Derlien

1. Sun-shine and rain, yes, both these must be,___ If from the seed shall grow forth a tree,___ But for my dar-ling two suns are nigh,___ So hush thy weep-ing, hush lul-la-by.___ Blow wind so light,___ Hush, lul-la-by,___ Sleep now, good-night.__

2. Eyes of thy mo-ther keep thee in sight,___ Eyes dear and lov-ing, suns of the night,___ Ev-en to pure hearts comes once a sigh,___ So hush thy weep-ing, hush lul-la-by.___ Hush, lul-la-by,___

3. Stars now are peep-ing, crad-led in peace___ Rocked in-to dream-land all cares shall cease,___ Sor-rows and troub-les they will pass by,___ Soon a new day dawns, hush lul-la-by.___

White Sheep

Unknown

Marlys Swinger

White sheep, white sheep, on a blue hill, When the wind stops You all stand still.

When the wind blows You walk a-way slow.— White sheep, white sheep, Where do you go?

The Earth Needs the Raindrops

J. Kartsch   A. Wagner

The earth needs the rain-drops,
The tree needs a lit-tle branch

The day needs a light,
Where the bird builds his nest,

And heav-en needs a lit-tle stars
And we need a lit-tle heart

When the day turns to night.
To love and to trust.

Good evening,

shining silver moon

Good Evening, Shining Silver Moon

German Folk Song

1. Good eve-ning, shin-ing sil-ver moon! Where sail you there so high?__
2. My beams shall play a-round the beds Where hap-py chil-dren sleep;__
3. A-cross the wand'-rer's lone-ly path I'll send my cheer-ing ray;__
4. I sail, dear child, a-cross the sky That I each night may show__

I go to shine where field and wood In dark-ness lie!_____
Where birds are hid in down-y nest, My watch I'll keep._____
I'll twin-kle where the mer-ry elves And fair-ies play._____
The Great Cre-a-tor's ten-der love For all be-low!_____

82

Little Brother in the Cradle

Words and Music by a seven-year old boy for his new baby brother.

Very gently

Lit-tle bro-ther in the cra-dle, Now lie still and quiet, my ba-by, A

lit-tle song I now am sing-ing, So that you will soon be sleep-ing. And then the an-gels

come so quiet-ly And fly a-round your bed so light-ly, They kiss your lit-tle

hand so soft-ly and cool your lit-tle cheeks so gent-ly, And love you ve-ry, ve-ry much.

Indian Lullaby

Henry W. Longfellow — Walter H. Aiken

1. Rock-a-bye, my lit-tle ow-let, In thy mos-sy, sway-ing nest,
2. Hush-a-bye, my lit-tle ow-let, Ma-ny voic-es sing to thee,

With thy lit-tle wood-land broth-ers, Close thine eyes and take thy rest. To whoo,__ to whoo,__ to
"Hush-a-bye," the wat-er whis-pers, "Hush!" re-plies the tall pine tree. To whoo,__ to whoo,__ to

whoo,__ to whoo.
whoo,__ to whoo.

3. Sleep, O Sleep, my little owlet,
Through our tent the moon shines bright,
Like a great eye it will watch thee,
Sleep till comes the morning light,
To whoo, to whoo,
To whoo, to whoo.

84

Little Red Bird

Manx Lullaby

Tenderly

Lit-tle red bird of the lone-ly moor, Lone-ly moor, lone-ly moor;

Lit-tle red bird of the lone-ly moor, O where did you sleep in the night?

1. Out on a gorse-bush dark and wide, Dark and wide, dark and wide,
2. Did I not sleep on a sway-ing briar, A sway-ing briar, a sway-ing briar?
3. Wrapp'd in two leaves I lay at ease, Lay at ease, lay at ease, As

Swift rain was fal-ling on ev-'ry side, O hard was my sleep last night.____
Toss-ing a-bout as the wind rose higher, O lit-tle I slept last night.____
sleeps the young babe on its mo-ther's knees, O sweet was my sleep last night.____

Sleep, My Duckling

Finnish Folk Song

Gently rocking

1. Sleep, my duck-ling in the rush-es While the winds are blow-ing.
2. Sleep, my duck-ling in the rush-es, Night winds rock you gent-ly.

1. Where is your fa-ther, where is your mo-ther To sing you in-to slum-ber?
2. Sun-shine will warm you, waves will cool you, God will care for and love you.

Heidschi Bumbeidschi

Old Bavarian Folk Song

1. *A-ber heid-schi bum beid-schi, small bro-ther___ Sleep soft-ly the hours while thy mo-ther___ Is
2. A-ber heid-schi bum beid-schi, sleep sweet-ly,___ The an-gels are com-ing to greet thee;___They'll

*Pronounced: Ah-ber highchee boom by chee.

leav-ing her dar-ling for an-gels to keep_And watch o'er her ba-by in dream-land a-sleep. Ab-er
wel-come you there for a ride in the sky_ A-cross the deep blue on a pon-y to fly. Ab-er

heid-schi bum-beid-schi, bum bum, (bum bum) A-ber heid-schi bum-beid-schi bum bum.___
heid-schi bum-beid-schi, bum bum, (bum bum) A-ber heid-schi bum-beid-schi bum bum.___

3. Aber heidschi bumbeidschi, in heaven
A pony snow white you'll be given,
And on it an angel
    with lantern so bright,
The loveliest star
    in the darkness of night.
Aber heidschi bumbeidschi bum bum,
Aber heidschi bumbeidschi bum bum.

4. The heidschi bumbeidschi comes riding,
My little one into sleep guiding,
He's taking him up
    to the star-dotted sky,
Good-night now, my baby,
    and sweet lullaby.
Aber heidschi bumbeidschi bum bum,
Aber heidschi bumbeidschi bum bum.

My Lantern

German

I Walk with My Little Lantern

Lively, gay   German

I walk with my lit-tle lan-tern, My lan-tern, my-self and I.___ Up
We walk with our lit-tle lan-terns, Our lan-terns so shin-y bright.___ We

yon-der bright lit-tle stars shine;___ Down here we're stars to the sky.___ The
wan-der through the dark-ness___ With wink-ing, twink-ling light.___ Like

new moon shines,___ The cat me-ows. * Eh!___ Eh!___ Eh!___ ** La-bum-mel, la bum-mel, la
stars that swing___ Are lan-terns we bring.

*Rhymes with 'bay'   **La boom-a-la boom-a-la bay

beh!___ Eh!___ Eh!___ Eh!___ La bum-mel, la bum-mel, la beh!

These two songs are from Germany where the children have the
lovely custom of walking and singing at night with lighted lanterns.

91

Wynken, Blynken, and Nod

Eugene Field

R. Houston Macdonald

With a gentle motion

1. Wyn - ken, Blyn - ken, and Nod one night__ Sailed off in a wood-en shoe,__
2. old moon laugh'd and sang a song, As they rocked in the wood-en shoe,__ And the
3. All night long their nets they threw To the stars in the twink-ling foam,__ Then
4. Wyn-ken and Blyn-ken are two lit-tle eyes,__ And Nod is a lit-tle head,__ And the

Sailed on a ri-ver of crys-tal light,__ In-to a sea of dew;__
wind that sped them all night long,__ Ruf-fled the waves of dew;__ The
down from the skies came the wood-en shoe, Bring-ing the fish-er-men home;__ 'Twas
wood-en shoe that sailed the skies __Is a wee one's trun-dle bed;__ So

93

Which Is the Way the Wind Blows?

Dreamily

Old Dutch Cradle Song

1. Which is the way the wind blows___ Ov-er the sil - ver sea?___
2. Which is the way the wind blows___ Ov-er the sil - ver sea?___
3. Which is the way the wind blows___ Ov-er the sil - ver sea?___

Bring-ing a ship for fa - ther And a gold - en dream for me.___
Bring-ing a gown for mo - ther And a sil - ver shoe for me.___
Bring-ing a moon for mo - ther And a ti - ny star for me.___

Far in the Wood

Anonymous

Flowing

Far in the wood you'll find a well With water deep and
And all a-round the lit-tle well Are se-ven love-ly

blue;_____ Who-ev-er drinks by moon-light clear, Ti - ri ti-ra ti-
trees,_____ They rock and sway and sing a song, Ti - ri ti-ra ti-

ra-la-la-la, Will live a thou-sand years,_____ Will live a thous-and years.
ra-la-la-la, And whis-per in the breeze,_____ And whis-per in the breeze.

And through the seven lovely trees
The evening wind will blow,
And down fall seven little dreams,
    Ti-ri, ti-ra, ti-ra-la-la-la,
My baby, all for you,
My baby, all for you.

Little Lambkin Sweet

Jane Tyson Clement

(for Abigail)

Marlys Swinger

Tenderly

1. Now the dark-ness creeps and my lamb-kin sleeps.___ Small stars
2. Day will come a-gain bring-ing sun or rain,___ Dais-ies
3. Now the dark-ness creeps and my lamb-kin sleeps___ Safe-ly

far a-way flick-er on and play___ Heav-en's games all night___ while your
at your feet, friend-ly dogs to meet,___ Balls to roll a-way,___ danc-ing
tucked a-way for a-noth-er day.___ May God's bless-ing rest___ by your

eyes shut tight,___ Lit-tle lamb-kin sweet, Lit-tle lamb-kin sweet.___
games to play,___ Lit-tle lamb-kin sweet, Lit-tle lamb-kin sweet.___
co-sy nest,___ Lit-tle lamb-kin sweet, Lit-tle lamb-kin sweet.___

Daisies

Frank Dempster Sherman

Winifred Dyroff

1. At eve-ning when I go to bed, I see the stars shine o-ver-head;
2. And of-ten while I'm dream-ing so, A-cross the sky the Moon will go,
3. For when at morn-ing I a-rise, There's not a star left in the skies;

They are the lit-tle dais-ies white That dot the mead-ow of the night.
It is a la-dy, sweet and fair, Who comes to gath-er dais-ies there.
She's picked them all and dropped them down In-to the mead-ows of the town.

Go to Sleep

Rockingly

American Folk Song

Go to sleep, go to sleep,___ Go to sleep, lit-tle ba-by,___ When you wake you shall

have___ A coach and six lit-tle hor-ses,___ Five lit-tle mice and three lit-tle rats,___ A

coach and six lit-tle hor-ses,___ Four lit-tle dogs___ and two lit-tle cats,___ A coach and six lit-tle

hors-es.___ Go to sleep, go to sleep,___ Go to sleep lit-tle ba-by.___

Little Donkey Close Your Eyes

Margaret Wise Brown

Marlys Swinger

1. Lit-tle don-key on the hill Stand-ing there so ve-ry still Mak-ing fa-ces at the skies, Lit-tle don-key close _____ your eyes.
2. Wild young birds that sweet-ly sing Curve your heads be-neath your wing; Dark night co-vers all the skies, Wild young birds now close _____ your eyes.
3. Old black cat down in the barn Keep-ing five small kit-tens warm. Let the wind blow in the skies, Dear old black cat close _____ your eyes.
4. Lit-tle child all tucked in bed Look-ing such a sleep-y head, Stars are qui-et in the skies, Lit-tle child now close _____ your eyes.

101

This is the Day!